Amanda Gorman

CHERRY LAKE PRESS

Published in the United States of America by Cherry Lake Publishing Group
Ann Arbor, Michigan
www.cherrylakepublishing.com

Reading Adviser: Beth Walker Gambro, MS, Ed., Reading Consultant, Yorkville, IL
Book Designer: Jennifer Wahi
Illustrator: Jeff Bane

Photo Credits: ©Monkey Business Images/Shutterstock, 5; ©Jersy/Shutterstock, 7; ©Library of Congress/ Wikimedia, 9; ©Stuart Ramson for United Nations Foundation/Wikimedia, 11; ©Modxka/Shutterstock, 13; ©Library of Congress/Wikimedia, 15, 22; ©Chairman of the Joint Chiefs of Staff/DOD Photo by Navy Petty Officer 1st Class Carlos M. Vazquez II/flickr, 17, 23; ©fitzcrittle/Shutterstock, 19; ©Kathy Hutchins/Shutterstock, 21; Cover, 1, 6, 14, 18, Jeff Bane; Various frames throughout, Shutterstock

Cherry Lake Press is an imprint of Cherry Lake Publishing Group.

Library of Congress Cataloging-in-Publication Data

Names: Briscoe, Eyrn, author. | Bane, Jeff, 1957- illustrator.
Title: Amanda Gorman / by Eyrn Briscoe ; illustrated by Jeff Bane.
Description: Ann Arbor, Michigan : Cherry Lake Publishing, [2022] | Series: My itty-bitty bio | Includes index.
Identifiers: LCCN 2021007969 (print) | LCCN 2021007970 (ebook) | ISBN 9781534196643 (hardcover) | ISBN 9781534196667 (paperback) | ISBN 9781534196650 (pdf) | ISBN 9781534196674 (ebook)
Subjects: LCSH: Gorman, Amanda, 1998---Juvenile literature. | African American women poets--Biography--Juvenile literature. | Poets, American--21st century--Biography--Juvenile literature.
Classification: LCC PS3607.O59774 Z55 2021 (print) | LCC PS3607.O59774 (ebook) | DDC 811/.6 [B]--dc23
LC record available at https://lccn.loc.gov/2021007969
LC ebook record available at https://lccn.loc.gov/2021007970

Printed in the United States of America
Corporate Graphics

My Story 4

Timeline. 22

Glossary .24

Index 24

About the author: Eyrn Briscoe grew up in Cleveland, Ohio. Eyrn finds joy in reading, creating, and doing yoga.

About the illustrator: Jeff Bane and his two business partners own a studio along the American River in Folsom, California, home of the 1849 Gold Rush. When Jeff's not sketching or illustrating for clients, he's either swimming or kayaking in the river to relax.

My name is Amanda Gorman. I was born March 7, 1998.

My mom raised me. She is an English teacher.

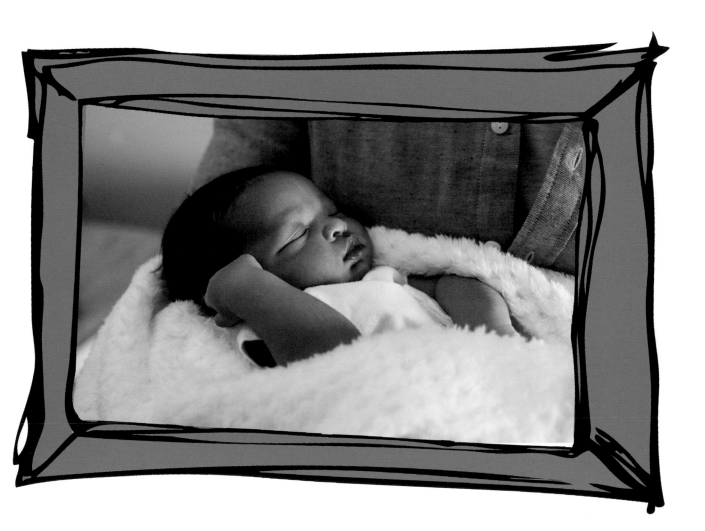

I fell in love with poetry. I love reading and writing.

What do you like to read and write?

Speaking was hard for me as a child.

It did not stop me. I was inspired.

What is your inspiration?

In 2013, I became a **United Nations Youth Delegate**.

I started a **nonprofit** called One Pen One Page.

It brings writing programs to children.

In 2017, I was the first-ever National Youth **Poet Laureate**.

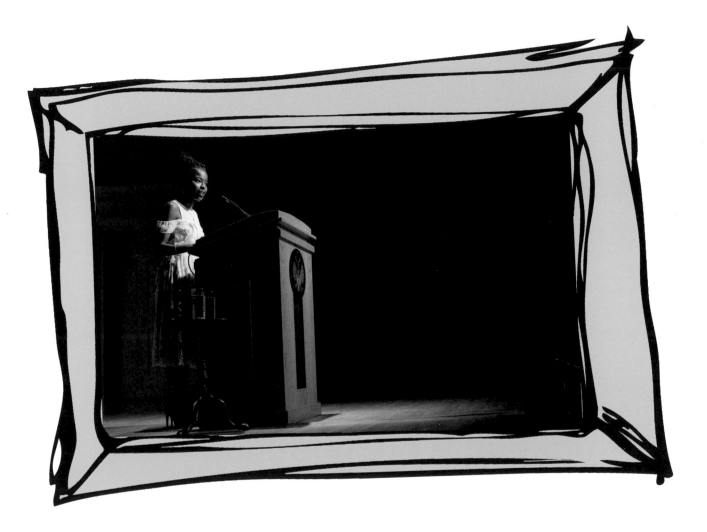

I spoke at a presidential **inauguration**. I made history. I read a poem I wrote.

I performed at the Super Bowl.
I honored people who helped
during the **pandemic**.

I've written books. I've inspired others.

One day, I would like to run for president. I want to continue to change the world.

What would you like to ask me?

2017

1990

Born
1998

2021

2090

glossary

inauguration (in-aw-gyuh-RAY-shuhn) a ceremony centered on the transition of a new national president into office

nonprofit (nahn-PRAH-fuht) not making or conducted primarily to make a profit

pandemic (pan-DEH-mik) a disease that has spread across the world

poet laureate (POH-uht LOR-ee-uht) an honorary position that a poet holds after being appointed by the government

United Nations Youth Delegate (yoo-NYE-tuhd NAY-shuhns YOOTH DEH-lih-guht) a young person who participates in United Nations meetings as a representative of the young people of their country

index

inauguration, 16
inspired, 8, 9, 20

National Youth Poet
    Laureate, 14
nonprofit, 12

pandemic, 18
poetry, 6, 14, 16

reading, 6, 7, 16

Super Bowl, 18

United Nations Youth
    Delegate, 10

writing, 6, 7, 12, 20